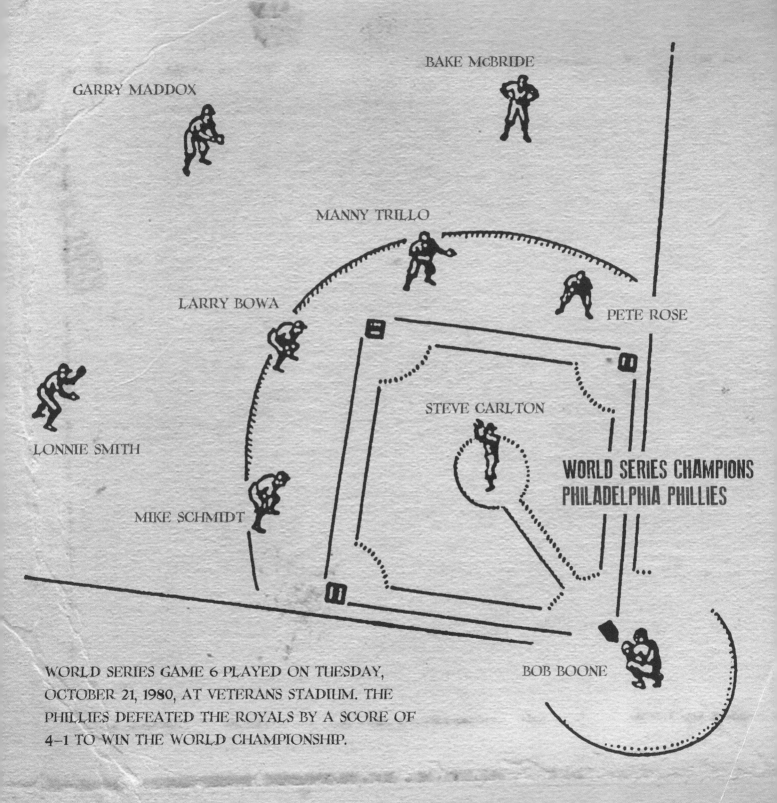

GARRY MADDOX

BAKE McBRIDE

MANNY TRILLO

LARRY BOWA

PETE ROSE

LONNIE SMITH

STEVE CARLTON

WORLD SERIES CHAMPIONS
PHILADELPHIA PHILLIES

MIKE SCHMIDT

BOB BOONE

WORLD SERIES GAME 6 PLAYED ON TUESDAY,
OCTOBER 21, 1980, AT VETERANS STADIUM. THE
PHILLIES DEFEATED THE ROYALS BY A SCORE OF
4–1 TO WIN THE WORLD CHAMPIONSHIP.

WORLD SERIES CHAMPIONS

PHILADELPHIA PHILLIES

SARA GILBERT

CREATIVE EDUCATION

Published by Creative Education
P.O. Box 227, Mankato, Minnesota 56002
Creative Education is an imprint of The Creative Company
www.thecreativecompany.us

Design and production by Blue Design (www.bluedes.com)
Art direction by Rita Marshall
Printed in the United States of America

Photographs by Getty Images (Dan Bigelow, Chicago History
Museum, Diamond Images, Focus on Sport, Drew Hallowell, Mark
Hirsch, Jed Jacobsohn, Mitchell Layton, Robert Leiter/MLB Photos,
Bob Levey, National Baseball Hall of Fame Library/MLB Photos,
Christian Petersen, Rich Pilling/MLB Photos, Louis Requena/
MLB Photos, Mark Rucker/Transcendental Graphics, George Silk/
Time & Life Pictures, Rick Stewart, Tony Tomsic/MLB Photos, Rob
Tringali/Sportschrome, Ron Vesely/MLB Photos)

Library of Congress Cataloging-in-Publication Data
Gilbert, Sara.
Philadelphia Phillies / Sara Gilbert.
p. cm. — (World series champions)
Includes bibliographical references and index.
Summary: A simple introduction to the Philadelphia Phillies major
league baseball team, including its start in 1883, its World Series
triumphs, and its stars throughout the years.
ISBN 978-1-60818-270-1
1. Philadelphia Phillies (Baseball team)—History—Juvenile
literature. I. Title.
GV875.P45G55 2013
796.357'640974811—dc23   2012004264

First edition
9 8 7 6 5 4 3 2 1

Cover: Pitcher Cliff Lee
Page 2: Pitcher Roy Halladay
Page 3: Shortstop Jimmy Rollins
Right: The Phillies in the 2008 World Series

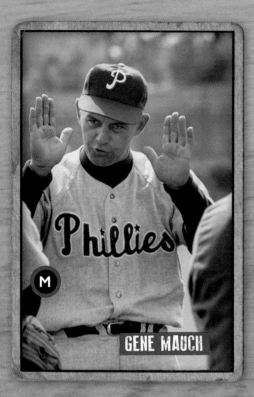

M

GENE MAUCH

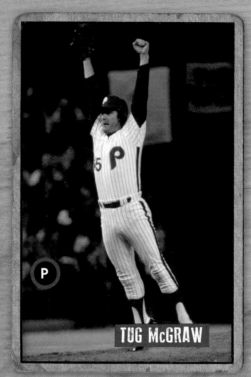

P

TUG McGRAW

CF

RITCHIE ASHBURN

RF

SAM THOMPSON

CF

CY WILLIAMS

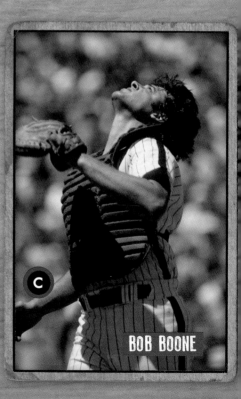

C

BOB BOONE

TABLE OF CONTENTS

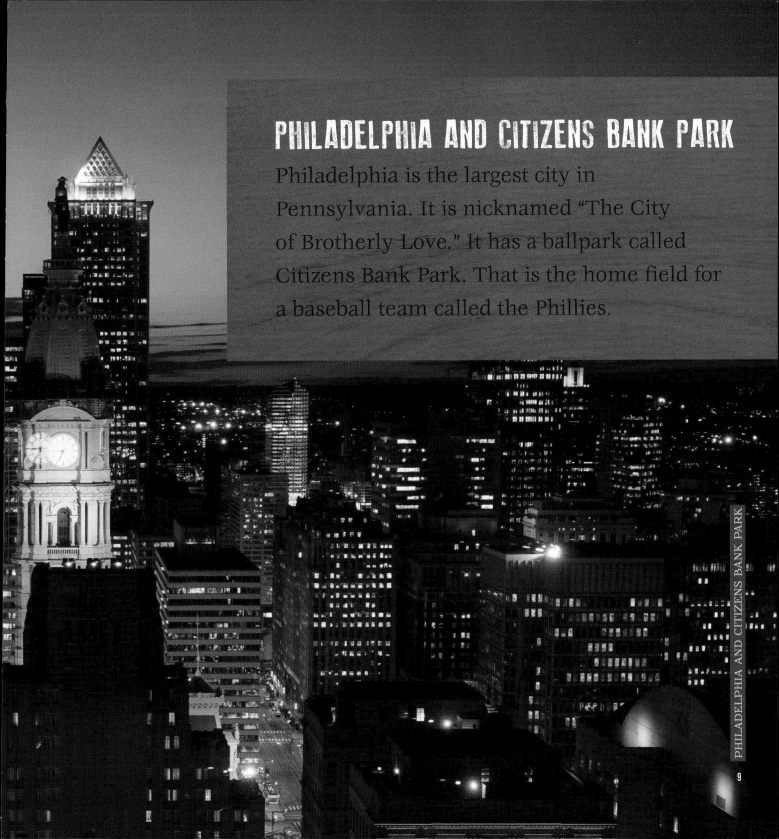

PHILADELPHIA AND CITIZENS BANK PARK

Philadelphia is the largest city in Pennsylvania. It is nicknamed "The City of Brotherly Love." It has a ballpark called Citizens Bank Park. That is the home field for a baseball team called the Phillies.

RIVALS AND COLORS

The Phillies are a major league baseball team. They play against the other 29 major-league teams to win the World Series and become world champions. The Phillies wear red and white uniforms. Their main **RIVALS** are the New York Mets.

LEFT FIELDER GREG LUZINSKI

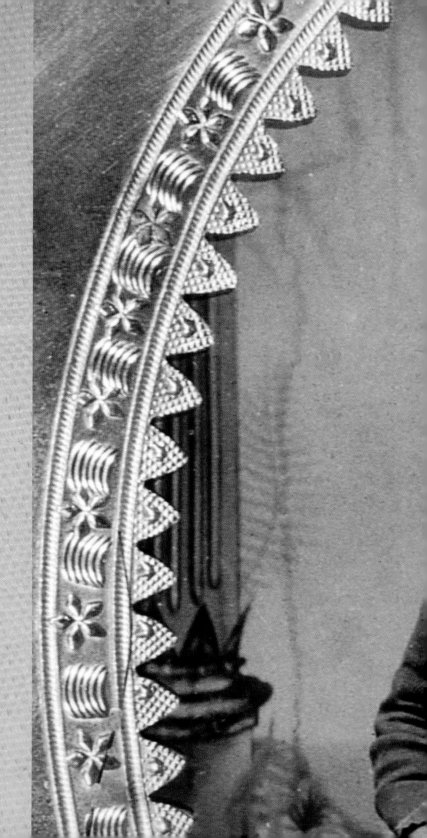

PHILLIES HISTORY

The Phillies played their first season in 1883. They were called the Quakers then. They won only 17 games that year, but they got better after that. In 1915, they won 90 games and made it to the World Series. But they lost.

For many years, the Phillies were known for hitting well but

PHILLIES PLAYERS IN 1886

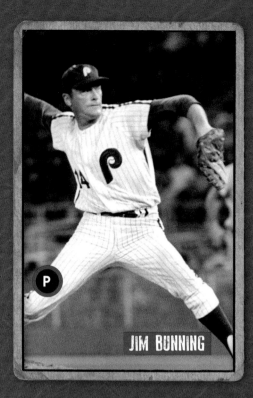

P

JIM BUNNING

SS

LARRY BOWA

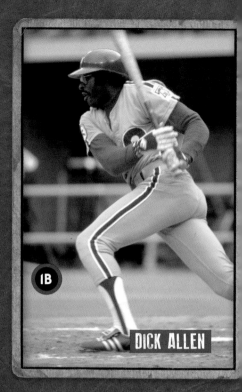

1B

DICK ALLEN

SS

JIMMY ROLLINS

2B

TONY TAYLOR

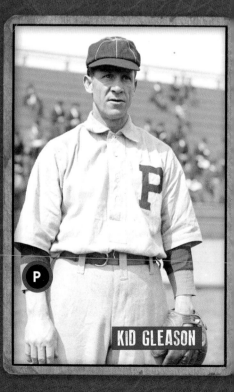

P

KID GLEASON

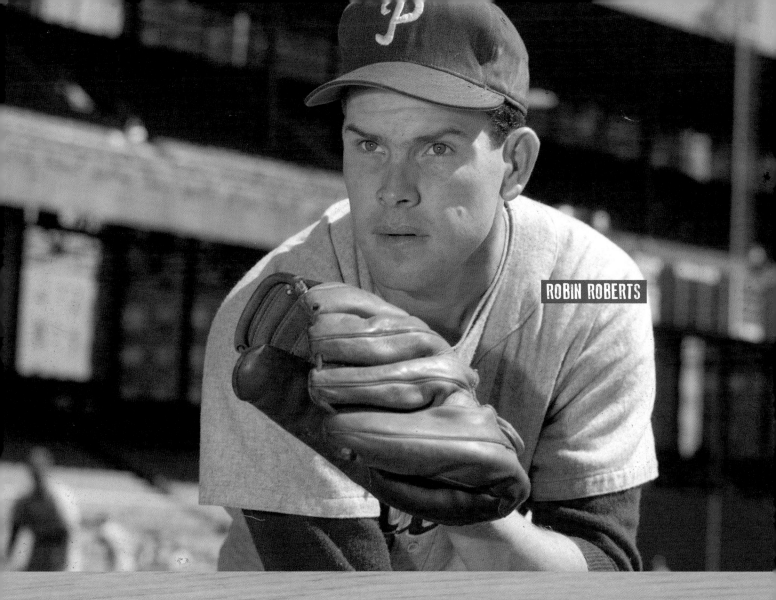

ROBIN ROBERTS

pitching poorly. That changed when pitcher Robin Roberts joined the team. In 1950, his fastballs helped the Phillies reach the World Series. But they lost again.

Pitcher Steve Carlton helped the Phillies return to the World Series in 1980. This time, they beat the Kansas City Royals to

STEVE CARLTON

win it. For the first time in the team's 97-year history, they were world champions!

The Phillies played in the World Series in 1983 and 1993 but lost. Then, in 2008, center fielder Shane Victorino helped them get back to the **PLAYOFFS**. The Phillies won their second world championship!

SHANE VICTORINO

GROVER CLEVELAND ALEXANDER

MIKE SCHMIDT

PHILLIES STARS

Pitcher Grover Cleveland Alexander was a Phillies star from 1911 to 1917. He was so good that his teammates called him "Alexander the Great." Outfielder Chuck Klein hit 243 home runs for Philadelphia. He won the Most Valuable Player award in 1932.

VERSATILE third baseman Mike Schmidt played hard for 18 years

PHILLIES STARS

19

in Philadelphia. Fans voted him the "Greatest Phillies Player Ever" in 1983. In 1989, star outfielder Lenny Dykstra joined the team. Fans loved his **HUSTLE**.

First baseman Ryan Howard hit a lot of home runs for Philadelphia starting in 2004. Fans hoped that he would keep slugging the ball over the fence and help the Phillies return to the World Series soon!

LENNY DYKSTRA

RYAN HOWARD

SECOND BASEMAN CHASE UTLEY

HOW THE PHILLIES GOT THEIR NAME

The owner of the Phillies wanted to name his team the Athletics. A team that used to play in Philadelphia had been named the Athletics, too. But another team was already using that name. So he decided to name the team the "Philadelphias" after its hometown. That was soon shortened to just Phillies.

ABOUT THE PHILLIES

First season: 1883

League/division: National League, East Division

World Series championships:

1980	*4 games to 2 versus Kansas City Royals*
2008	*4 games to 1 versus Tampa Bay Rays*

Phillies Web site for kids:

http://mlb.mlb.com/phi/fan_forum/kids_index.jsp

Club MLB:

http://web.clubmlb.com/index.html

GLOSSARY

HUSTLE — moving fast or trying hard to get a job done

PLAYOFFS — all the games (including the World Series) after the regular season that are played to decide who the champion will be

RIVALS — teams that play extra hard against each other

VERSATILE — able to do many different things well

INDEX